Side Effects

U. A. FANTHORPE

HARRY CHAMBERS/PETERLOO POETS

First published in 1978
by Harry Chambers/Peterloo Poets
Treovis Farm Cottage, Upton Cross, Liskeard, Cornwall PL14 5BQ

Reprinted 1979, 1982, 1984

ISBN 0 905291 14 X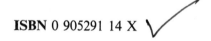

Printed in Great Britain by
Latimer Trend & Company Ltd

ACKNOWLEDGMENTS are due to the editors of *Encounter*, *Intak'* (Yorkshire Poets), *Meridian*, *New Poetry*, *Poetry Review*, and *Use of English*, in whose pages some of these poems first appeared. Some of these poems have also appeared in the following anthologies: *New Poetry 2* (Arts Council of Great Britain), *P.E.N. New Poems, 1977-78*, *Poetry In The Seventies* (Rondo), and *Poetry Dimension Annual 5*.

'Men On Allotments' won First Prize in the *Michael Johnson Memorial Poetry Competition*, 1976.

'My Brother's House' won Second Prize in the *Stroud International Poetry Competition*, 1976.

'Not My Best Side' won Second Prize in *Phoenix* magazine's *Poem About A Painting* competition, 1975.

The cover illustration of Uccello's *S. George and the Dragon* is reproduced by courtesy of the Trustees, The National Gallery, London.

5

For Rosemarie Bailey

Contents

The List

Flawlessly typed, and spaced
At the proper intervals,
Serene and lordly, they pace
Along tomorrow's list
Like giftbearers on a frieze.

In tranquil order, arrayed
With the basic human equipment—
A name, a time, a number—
They advance on the future.

Not more harmonious who pace
Holding a hawk, a fish, a jar
(The customary offerings)
Along the Valley of the Kings.

Tomorrow these names will turn nasty,
Senile, pregnant, late,
Handicapped, handcuffed, unhandy,
Muddled, moribund, mute,

Be stained by living. But here,
Orderly, equal, right,
On the edge of tomorrow, they pause
Like giftbearers on a frieze

With the proper offering,
A time, a number, a name.
I am the artist, the typist;
I did my best for them.

The Watcher

I am a watcher; and the things I watch
Are birds and love.

Not the more common sorts of either kind.
Not sparrows, nor

Young couples. Such successful breeds are blessed
By church and state,

Surviving in huge quantities. I like
The rare Welsh kite,

Clinging to life in the far Radnor hills;
The tiny wren,

Too small for winter; and the nightingale,
Chased from her home

By bulldozers and speculating men.
In human terms,

The love I watch is rare, its habitat
Concealed and strange.

The very old, the mad, the failures. These
Have secret shares

Of loving and of being loved. I can't
Lure them with food,

Stare at them through binoculars, or join
Societies

That will preserve them. Birds are easier
To do things for.

But love is so persistent, it survives
With no one's help

Like starlings in Trafalgar Square, cut off
By many miles

From life-supporting trees, finding their homes
On dirty roofs,

So these quiet lovers, miles from wedding bells,
Cherish their odd

And beastly dears with furtive fondling hands
And shamefaced looks,

Finding their nesting-place in hospitals
And prison cells.

Jobdescription: Medical Records

Innocence is important, and order.
You need have no truck with the
Seamy insides of notes, where blood
And malignant growths and indelicate

Photographs wait to alarm. We like
To preserve innocence. You will
Be safe here, under the permanent
Striplighting. (Twenty-four hours cover.

Someone is always here. Our notes
Require constant company.) No
Patients, of course. The porter comes
And goes, but doesn't belong. With

His hairless satyr's grin, he knows
More than is suitable. Your conversation
Should concern football and television.
You may laugh at his dirty jokes,

But not tell any. Operations
Are not discussed here. How, by
The way, is your imagination?
Poorly, I hope. We do not encourage

Speculation in clerks. We prefer you
To think of patients not as people, but
Digits. That makes it much easier. Our system
Is terminal digit filing. If you

Are the right type for us, you will be
Unconscious of overtones. The contrasting
Weights of histories (puffy
For the truly ill, thin and clean

For childhood's greenstick fractures)
Will not concern you. You will use
The Death Book as a matter of routine
Our shelves are tall, our files heavy. Have you

A strong back and a good head for heights?

Specialist

This specialist
Holds himself stiffly upright, lest
He spill a drop of his precious
Ichor.

Rose-cheeked, dwarf-high,
He runs along the corridors,
Humming the more obvious
Arias.

He is brave with
Convicted murderers, female
Thugs, aggressive juveniles, but
Dare not

Raise his eyes when
His inferiors cross his path.
He knows no private words for private chat.
His fog-

Horn voice only
Gives orders, nothing subtle can
Be bellowed through the force-eight gale
Appliance.

His heart is in
His dinghy, where he can be cock
Of the whole thwart, no space there for
Subordinates.

I am ashamed
To be annoyed by his brutal
Rejection of delicacy
When he

Pours out so much
Of his ichor, modulates so
Touchingly his loud-hailer, for
His landsick patients.

For Saint Peter

I have a good deal of sympathy for you, mate,
Because I reckon that, like me, you deal with the outpatients.

Now the inpatients are easy, they're cowed by the nurses
(In your case, the angels) and they know what's what in the set-up.

They know about God (in my case Dr Snow) and all His little fads,
And if there's any trouble with them, you can easily scare them
    rigid

Just by mentioning His name. But outpatients are different.
They bring their kids with them, for one thing, and that creates a
    wrong atmosphere.

They have shopping baskets, and buses to catch. They cry, or knit,
Or fall on the floor in convulsions. In fact, Saint Peter,

If you know what I mean, they haven't yet learned
How to be reverent.

Linguist

The smashed voice roars inside the ruined throat
Behind the mangled face. Voice of the wild,
Voice of a warthog calling to his mates,

Wordless, huge-volumed, sad. We can't make out
A meaning (though his wife can). Solitary
He sits, shrouded in his vast noise. How strange

To make so much, none of it any use
To fragile human ears, except to mis-
Inform. For we all make the obvious

And wrong deduction: *this poor chap is mad.*
He doesn't talk like us. He can't be sane.
And yet he is. Look in his serious eyes;

He understands. Reads magazines. He bawls
Obliterated meanings at his wife.
O yes, she says, *a sundial would be nice.*

That's what he'd like. A silent clock that speaks
The solemn language of the sun to grass
And garden-lovers with a turn for sums.

Casehistory: Julie (encephalitis)

She stands between us. Her dress
Is zipped up back to front.
She has been crying her eyes
Dark. Her legs are thinner than legs.

She is importunate.

I'm not mental, am I?
Someone told me I was mental,
But I lost me memory
'Cos our dad died.
It don't make sense though, do it?
After I've been a nurse.

Her speech is nothing.

If I been rude, I apologise.
I lost me memory
'Cos I had the flu, didn't I?
I thought it was 'cos our dad died, see.
But it was 'cos I had the flu.

What imports this song?

Married? O god forgive me.
Who to? let's be fair,
If you're getting married,
You ought to know the man.
O, not Roy!
I didn't marry him, did I?
I must be mental.
I'll do meself in.

There is a willow.

He was different to my brothers.
God forgive me for saying this,
He was like a woman.
Children? O god, please help me,
Please do, god.

O rose of May.

I'm getting better,
The doctor told me so,
As god's me witness, touch wood.
O, I am hungry.
I hope you don't mind me asking,
Where's the toilet to?

Do you see this, O God?

What about me dad?
Me dad's not gone, is he?

19

Casehistory: Alison (head injury)

(She looks at her photograph)

I would like to have known
My husband's wife, my mother's only daughter.
A bright girl she was.

Enmeshed in comforting
Fat, I wonder at her delicate angles.
Her autocratic knee

Like a Degas dancer's
Adjusts to the observer with airy poise,
That now lugs me upstairs

Hardly. Her face, broken
By nothing sharper than smiles, holds in its smiles
What I have forgotten

She knows my father's dead,
And grieves for it, and smiles. She has digested
Mourning. Her smile shows it.

I, who need reminding
Every morning, shall never get over what
I do not remember.

Consistency matters.
I should like to keep faith with her lack of faith,
But forget her reasons.

Proud of this younger self,
I assert her achievements, her A levels,
Her job with a future.

Poor clever girl! I know,
For all my damaged brain, something she doesn't:
I am her future.

A bright girl she was.

Patience Strong

Everyone knows her name. Trite calendars
Of rose-nooked cottages or winding ways
Display her sentiments in homespun verse
Disguised as prose. She has her tiny niche
In women's magazines, too, tucked away
Among the recipes or near the end
Of some perennial serial. Her theme
Always the same: rain falls in every life,
But rainbows, bluebirds, spring, babies or God
Lift up our hearts. No doubt such rubbish sells.
She must be feathering her inglenook.
Genuine poets seldom coin the stuff,
Nor do they flaunt such aptly bogus names.
Their message is oblique; it doesn't fit
A pocket diary's page; nor does it pay.

One day in epileptic out-patients,
A working-man, a fellow in his fifties,
Was feeling bad. I brought a cup of tea.
He talked about his family and job:
His dad was in the Ambulance Brigade;
He hoped to join, but being epileptic,
They wouldn't have him. *Naturally*, he said,
With my disease, I'd be a handicap.
But I'd have liked to help. He sucked his tea,
Then from some special inner pocket brought
A booklet muffled up in cellophane,
Unwrapped it gently, opened at a page—
Characteristic cottage garden, seen
Through chintzy casement windows. Underneath
Some cosy musing in the usual vein,
And *See*, he said, *this is what keeps me going.*

From The Remand Centre

Eleven stone and nineteen years of want
Flex inside Koreen. Voices speak to her
In dreams of love. She needs it like a fag,
Ever since Mum, who didn't think her daft,
Died suddenly in front of her. She holds
Her warder lovingly with powerful palms,
Slings head upon her shoulders, cries *Get lost*,
Meaning *I love you*, and her blows caress.

Woman's Touch

Her mother's flower arrangements humanise
The hospital. Outpatients like to see
Brush-headed teazels, beech leaves' blue disguise,
The round transparent heads of honesty.
No reek of ether here, no hint of blood;
Wall-to-wall carpets and two fat, spayed cats,
Somerset gardener, apple-trees in bud,
Healthy inpatients wearing woolly hats.
We operate on nothing trivial here;
We only amputate the anxious brain,
Excising cells until the knack of fear
Oozes away. That's why we're so urbane.
Our floral decor hints that you will find
Wall-to-wall carpeting within the mind.

After Visiting Hours

Like gulls they are still calling—
I'll come again Tuesday. Our Dad
Sends his love. They diminish, are gone.
Their world has received them,

As our world confirms us. Their debris
Is tidied into vases, lockers, minds.
We become pulses; mouthpieces
Of thermometers and bowels.

The trolley's rattle dispatches
The last lover. Now we can relax
Into illness, and reliably abstracted
Nurses will straighten our sheets,

Reorganize our symptoms. Outside,
Darkness descends like an eyelid.
It rains on our nearest and dearest
In car-parks, at bus-stops.

Now the bed-bound rehearse
Their repertoire of movements,
The dressing-gowned shuffle, clutching
Their glass bodies.

Now siren voices whisper
From headphones, and vagrant
Doctors appear, wreathed in stethoscopes
Like South Sea dancers.

All's well, all's quiet as the great
Ark noses her way into night,
Caulked, battened, blessed for her trip,
And behind, the gulls crying.

Earthed

Not precisely, like a pylon or
A pop-up toaster, but in a general
Way, stuck in the mud.

Not budding out of it like gipsies,
Laundry lashed to a signpost, dieting on
Nettles and hedgehogs,

Not lodged in its layers like badgers,
Tuned to the runes of its home-made walls, wearing
Its shape like a skin,

Not even securely rooted, like
Tribesmen tied to the same allotment, sure of
The local buses,

But earthed for all that, in the chalky
Kent mud, thin sharp ridges between wheel-tracks, in
Surrey's wild gravel,

In serious Cotswold uplands, where
Limestone confines the verges like yellow teeth,
And trees look sideways.

Everything from the clouds downwards holds
Me in its web, like the local newspapers,
Routinely special,

Or Somerset belfries, so highly
Parochial that Gloucestershire has none, or
Literate thrushes,

Conscientiously practising the
Phrases Browning liked, the attitude Hughes noticed,
Or supermarkets

Where the cashiers' rudeness is native
To the district, though the bread's not, or gardens,
Loved more than children,

Bright with resourcefulness and smelling
Of rain. This narrow island charged with echoes
And whispers snares me.

Stanton Drew

First you dismantle the landscape.
Take away everything you first
Thought of. Trees must go,
Roads, of course, the church,
Houses, hedges, livestock, a wire
Fence. The river can stay,
But loses its stubby fringe
Of willows. What do you
See now? Grass, the circling
Mendip rim, with its notches
Fresh, like carving. A sky
Like ours, but empty along
Its lower levels. And earth
Stripped of its future, tilted
Into meaning by these stones,
Pitted and unemphatic. Recreate them.
They are the most permanent
Presences here, but cattle, weather,
Archaeologists have rubbed against them.
Still in season they will
Hold the winter sun poised
Over Maes Knoll's white cheek,
Chain the moon's footsteps to
The pattern of their dance.
Stand inside the circle. Put
Your hand on stone. Listen
To the past's long pulse.

Owlpen Manor

I am folded among my terraces
Like an old dog half asleep.
The sunlight tickles my chimneys.

I have never cared for grandeur.
This narrow handcarved valley fits
My casual autocracy. But I hold

What's mine. The long, undistinguished
Dynasty of Cotswold gentlemen,
Who never married cleverly, and made

Only a modest fortune in Ireland,
Suited my fancy. Owlpens, Daunts
And Stoughtons, I charmed them to a happy

Apathy. Even Margaret, my ghost of Anjou,
Pacing my Great Chamber in her high-crowned hat,
Knowing that tomorrow is Tewkesbury,

Walks in benevolence. My floorboards creak
In their infinite adjustment to time.
I have outlasted my successor on the hill,

I am permanent as the muted roar
Of white pigeons in my barn, as the drift
Of dry leaves in my ancient garden.

Brympton d'Evercy

1. THE PRIEST'S HOUSE

You can see they have lived close
To humanity for a long time. That numbed look,
Those finger furrows, take time to grow.
Casualties of the annual offensive
Between the treacly clay of Somerset,
The obstinate earthy hands of labourers,
They recline here now, stiffly at ease.

We are what they achieved. The hay
Raked, hedges laid, milk scoured, rats
Trapped, eels skinned, clothes scrubbed, earth
Dug by these laborious tools, with their
Immense genealogies and no future,
Resulted in us. Now, mud scraped off,
They find themselves suddenly rare.

The blacksmith, dairymaid, wheelwright,
Ditcher, haytrusser and shepherd have all
Stepped into the dark, but these slow, brutal things,
These hammers, bits, castrators, pitchforks,
This table on which dynasties of pigs
Have bled into the grain, these tired hats
Lasted. Now they inspect us, their artifacts.

The rain knocks on the roof. We feel
Fragile, apologetic. This elaborate world,
Which ended so suddenly that the cider press
Smells still of apples, watches mutely,
Knowing more about local weather than
We do. Furtively we sprint ten wet yards
Of grass to the chapel.

2. THE CHAPEL

Whose consecrated air smells different,
Warm and encouraging. This place, perhaps,
Retains a tender feeling for mankind.
But no. We found it wasn't that at all:
Just central heating, on for Evensong.

Three people lay there, all too beautiful
To be disturbed. The whiskered knight, encased
In scales like a huge salmon, held a pose
Gymnastically graceful and absurd.
A nervous lion peered behind his feet.

The rains of time had run the lady's dogs
(One at each heel) into her marble skirt,
But still her thick stone lips were sensual,
The wimple horning on her rigid brows
Still made it clear her faded blood was blue.

The solemn forehead and devoted eyes
Of the long priest focussed their holy thought
Upon a mass of stone between his hands,
Substitute for the chalice time had drowned.
He was too much in love to notice us.

3. THE GARDEN

There is no room for us
Here. The past is too solid,
Too finished. The dead

Do not want us, except
As admirers. There are no
Cracks in their surface

For us to set root in.
But outside shining young vines
Grow green in the wet.

Coire Dubh

If I stand still, I can hear only
The river's hollow comment, the bright
Interjection of the stonechat.
Room for you here, in a land scoured
Fit for sheep, eagles, deer; among
These humps and cones, these acres
Of glowing uneloquent water.

You are what they are looking for,
These hills, heaving unendingly their brutal
Heads, poring over each other's purple
Shoulders and white heads, unendingly
Watching for something, though I
Am seen, too; and the jet's
Mechanical shadow.

You, who are looked for, are the ones
Who are not here. Only
A caretaker lot, offering bed
And breakfast: frying Scotsmen,
Foresters, roadmen and surly girls
Ambitious for jobs in Oban.
The only poets left are headmasters
And civil servants,

And the English, whose temperate
Home-made syntax can't accommodate
This empty disorderly landscape.
Poets were flushed out of Scotland,
And who else speaks mountains?
Who else knows the heather's logic,
The corrie's semantics?

Selfconsciously our alien tongues
Baptise Ben Sausage and Ben Goitre,
Formal peaks, whose many-vowelled names
Hang about them, beautiful and personal
As clouds, and like clouds
Are unspoken. We are not the ones.
We tramp where you should live

In your jolly, squalid hovels,
Children of Big Mary of the Songs
(Seventeen stone singing-weight)
And Alasdair son of the Minister
Of Islandfinnan in Moidart; children
Of hereditary bards who composed in the dark,
With boulders on their bellies.

Who are not here. Whose absence
Sings louder than the stonechat
And the crunch of climbing boots,
Louder than the clicks of your dumb
And glossy descendants, in computer
Rooms, by cash registers, consuming
The fattening cake of exile.

Campsite: Maentwrog

This field contains the modest apparatus
Of suburb life, incubating under
Separate bell-jars, hurricane lamp-lit.

We observe it. Domesticated mum
In the permanent apron, and dad, reverting
In the wild to a feral state,

Shirt-sleeved, morose. The quarrelling lovers
Rained on, in the car, by dashboard-light.
He pitched the tent alone; they left at dawn.

Children fetching milk and water, making
Work a ritual, like games, and playing
Only with children from respectable tents.

The flat-capped fisherman, working his punctual
Day-shift on the river, whose dog
Knew to expect him at tea-time. And you

And me, patrolling the domestic purlieus,
Getting on with knitting and letters,
All of us practising our characteristic selves,

Despite the grass, and the apologetically
Insistent rain. Abroad we should be
Other, conforming to the strangeness

Of bread and air. Here we are just
Ourselves forced under glass. You have to pay more
For expensive weather. This is a cheap country.

The West Front At Bath

The headscarfed tourists in the comfy shoes
Obediently make their scheduled pause
Among the pigeons. Sun and stone confuse
The rhythm of their uninformed applause.
Where are we now? Would it be Bath, perhaps?
Five o'clock deftly shoots its slanted gleam
Across their eyes. A thoughtless pigeon claps
His wings. This moment is as much a dream
As Jacob's nightmare on the Abbey wall,
Alive with straining angels, who with wing
Correctly folded, desperately crawl
Along their monstrous ladder. Evening
Distorts their poise. Above it all sits God,
Watching the dreams, and finding both kinds odd.

The Quiet Grave
(*for Cecil Sharp*)

Underground Rome waited solidly
In stone patience. Orpheus might lose
A beast or two, cracked apart by roots
Of brambled centuries, but still
Foundations lasted, knowing, like the princess,
That one day a ferret and a boy
Exploring a rabbithole would find an empire.

But this was a kingdom that lived

Some kinds of earth are reliable. The black
Peat of Somerset, and Norfolk mud
That tenderly cradled the deathship's spectral
Longrotted timbers. Some kinds of dryasdust
Air, too, responsibly cherish papyrus.

But this was a kingdom that lived
In the living air

Who held the keys of the kingdom?
Unfriendly old men in workhouses;
Bedridden ninety-year-olds terrorized
By highhanded grandchildren; gipsy women
With the long memories of the illiterate;
Old sailors who could sing only
Within sound of the sea. These
Held the keys of the kingdom.

Where was the kingdom?
The kingdom was everywhere. Under the noses
Of clerics devoted to folklore it lived
Invisibly, in gardens, in fields and kitchens,
In the servants' quarters. No one could find it
But those who were in it already.

When was the kingdom?
The kingdom was while women washed
And men broke stones. It was
Intervals in birdscaring; between
A cup too low and a cup
Too high; when a great-grandfather
Sang like a lark. Then
Was the kingdom.

Who cared for the kingdom?
An old woman gathering stones,
Who seized Sharp by his gentle-
Manly lapels, blowing her song into his mind
Through wrinkled gums. A surly chap
In Bridgwater Union, holding
Sharp's hand between his own grim bones,
Tears falling on all three. These
Cared for the kingdom.

What were the treasures of the kingdom?
Scraps of other worlds, prized
For their strangeness. A derrydown and a heyho,
And a rue dum day and a fol the diddle dee.
These were the treasures of the kingdom.

Who were the heirs of the kingdom?
The kingdom had no heirs, only
A younger generation that winked
At senility's music, and switched on the gramophone.

What was the end of the kingdom?
Massed choirs of the Federation
Of Women's Institutes filling
The Albert Hall; laconic
Improper poetry improved
For the benefit of schools;
Expansion of the Folk Song Industry. These
Were the end of the kingdom.

For this was a kingdom that lived
In the dying air

Not My Best Side

I
Not my best side, I'm afraid.
The artist didn't give me a chance to
Pose properly, and as you can see,
Poor chap, he had this obsession with
Triangles, so he left off two of my
Feet. I didn't comment at the time
(What, after all, are two feet
To a monster?) but afterwards
I was sorry for the bad publicity.
Why, I said to myself, should my conqueror
Be so ostentatiously beardless, and ride
A horse with a deformed neck and square hoofs?
Why should my victim be so
Unattractive as to be inedible,
And why should she have me literally
On a string? I don't mind dying
Ritually, since I always rise again,
But I should have liked a little more blood
To show they were taking me seriously.

II
It's hard for a girl to be sure if
She wants to be rescued. I mean, I quite
Took to the dragon. It's nice to be
Liked, if you know what I mean. He was
So nicely physical, with his claws
And lovely green skin, and that sexy tail,
And the way he looked at me,
He made me feel he was all ready to
Eat me. And any girl enjoys that.
So when this boy turned up, wearing machinery,
On a really *dangerous* horse, to be honest,
I didn't much fancy him. I mean,
What was he like underneath the hardware?
He might have acne, blackheads or even
Bad breath for all I could tell, but the dragon—

38

Well, you could see all his equipment
At a glance. Still, what could I do?
The dragon got himself beaten by the boy,
And a girl's got to think of her future.

III
I have diplomas in Dragon
Management and Virgin Reclamation.
My horse is the latest model, with
Automatic transmission and built-in
Obsolescence. My spear is custom-built,
And my prototype armour
Still on the secret list. You can't
Do better than me at the moment.
I'm qualified and equipped to the
Eyebrow. So why be difficult?
Don't you want to be killed and/or rescued
In the most contemporary way? Don't
You want to carry out the roles
That sociology and myth have designed for you?
Don't you realise that, by being choosy,
You are endandering job-prospects
In the spear- and horse-building industries?
What, in any case, does it matter what
You want? You're in my way.

Palimpsest

Once the surface of the ground has been
The sidelong eyes of dawn and twilight
disturbed, the effect is, for all practical
catch in the net of their long shadows
purposes, permanent: the perfect
what is no longer there: grass offers
vestigia of a temple, as
its mute sermon on earth's derangement,
easily discernible in the
invisible and indelible
corn as on paper.
as children's hatred.

Some Modernisation Needed

It wasn't inhospitable, exactly.
Preoccupied, perhaps. We didn't fit.
Our voices sounded gross, uncertain footsteps
Disturbed its poise. Side-set above the road,
Its four mild windows (two upstairs, two down)
Gazed south along the garden. Odds and ends
Of someone's life still hung around: a tin
Of Ajax in the kitchen, a tall-stalked
Geranium with little thirsty leaves,
And torn net curtains in the living room.

Despite its apathy it parted us.
You saw its future, on some August night,
Extended, painted, lived in, flushed with food,
Voices and flowers. Convivially chairs
Had clustered on the terrace. Someone played
These Foolish Things. Coffee, cigars and stock
Infused the air. This was how it would be.

The present held me in its frosted fist.
The house stayed sad and small, and smelt of cold.
Someone was dying upstairs in a slow
Damp-sheeted bed. The garden had turned strange.
The smell of its depression filtered through
Cracks in the window frames. The dying nose
Knew the sour drift of couchgrass, sliding sly,
Plaiting itself across the garden paths,
The whiff of mouldy blackberries, the thick
Polleny stink of asters run to seed.

We stood locked in our independent dreams,
Wondering why they weren't the same. The house
Shuffled its temperament between us both,
Equivocally fair. We took the key
Back to the agent, never talked of it,
The only house of all the ones we saw
To survey us, and keep its findings dark.

41

My Brother's House

Stood, like a fairytale, at the start
Of a wood. Vague fogs of bluebells
Absentmindedly invested it in summer.

Curdled dollops of snow
Flopped slowly in winter from invisible
Outstretched branches of firtrees.

The wood was a real wood, and
You could get lost in it. The trees
Had no names or numbers.

Jays, foxes and squirrels
Lived there. Also an obelisk in an odd
Corner, where nobody went.

The road to my brother's house
Had an air of leading nowhere. Visitors
Retreated, thinking of their back axles.

Blackberries and fifty-seven varieties
Of weeds had their eye on the garden.
Every year they shrivelled in flame,

Every day they returned unemphatic,
Not bothering to flaunt so
Easy a triumph. There was no garage

To uphold suburban standards, only
A shed where bicycles cowered among drips.
Indoors, all doors were always open

Or else jammed. Having a bath
Invited crowds, not just of spiders. Cats
Landed on chests with a thump and a yowl

In mid-dream. Overhead the patter of tiny
Paws or dense whirring of wings.
There were more humans around, too,

Than you quite expected, living furtive
Separate lives in damp rooms. Meals, haphazard
And elaborate, happened when, abandoning hope,

You had surrendered to bread
And butter. Massed choirs sang solidly
Through the masses of Haydn. Shoppers

Returned from forays with fifteen
Kinds of liversausage and no sugar.
When the family left, rats, rain and nettles

Took over instantly. I regret the passing
Of my brother's house. It was like living in Rome
Before the barbarians.

Rite

Foreign ground. It dips
Polished in every direction.

I long for squatter's rights
In a hymn book and part of a pew.
Snug C of E, where our fathers
Dozed anticipating roast beef, while shepherds
Slept by dogs, and Squire snored
At his private fireside, rousing
To contradict Rector. What one expects.

Here derelicts fling themselves down,
Agilely abject, and kiss the dirty lips
Of a picture. Untidily genuflecting
They visit the talkative candles. Saints
With flexible necks and symbolic fingers
Amble through goldleaf on impractical feet.
Ikons are scarfed like football crowds.

I stand in an uncommitted way
By the bookstall. Half the texts are Greek.

No choir. No priest, bell, book.
For landmark, the more desperate psalms,
Chanted in an even tenor which
Draws death's sting. No hymns,
But an impromptu hilarious
Madrigal group (three beards and one
Long skirt) intone delicately,

Guessing the note, dropping the music
Between tunes, and giggling
In harmony. This could go on
For ever. The derelicts
With random passion abase themselves.
Candles ebb. There is no heating.
My feet hurt.

In this holy web, where one-
Dimensional saints and floundering
Souls are safe together, I
Can find no place to be.
The polished floor caves in,
The smoke comes through.

Carol Concert

Before the ice has time to form
On the carparked windscreens, before
A single carol has announced itself,
The performance happens.
(sing lullaby virgin noel)

These sculptured hairdos, these fairy-
Tale dresses, gothic embraces—
Sophie, long time no see! —are they
The approved offering
(sing lullaby virgin noel)

To the dull obligatory
Young men, whose correct accent, tie
And sex are paraded like expensive
Perfume? Or is it friends
(sing lullaby virgin noel)

Who get this oblation? Known once
Sweaty, tearful, giggling, asleep,
In the undesigning equality
Of youth, now moving high
(sing lullaby virgin noel)

Into the difficult heavens
Of Hotel Management in Kent,
Of sitting Oxbridge, of getting married?
In the carpark ice forms,
(sing lullaby virgin noel)

In the hall inarticulate
Strange friendships falter. *The standard
Of singing* (they say) *has gone down. They must
Be missing us.* Prefects
(sing lullaby virgin noel)

Like angels watch with wondering eyes.
Next year perhaps they too will sport
Long curtain fabric skirts and Afro hair,
But their present faces
(sing lullaby virgin noel)

Deny complicity. The young
Bored man says he's having a ball,
While the choir with the innocent mouths
Of singers cry
Lullaby, virgin, noel.

Sir John

Bluff voices echo round his balding dome,
His deaf dead father's, and his wellborn wife's
Horsewoman's accent. With a docile thrill
Cosily he surrenders. His aplomb
Encompasses emotion's deshabille.

Fierce music echoes in his ears' canals,
Minor Victorians, Ancient and Mod.
Respectfully he hears, he doffs his old
Peculiar hat. But meanwhile something odd
Waylays the metre, and its lilt appals.

Dark-brown triforia enchant his mild
And baggy eyes, a Butterfield reredos,
Seaweedy seasons in a Cornishscape,
Or flying, buttressed legs of hot lacrosse-
Devoted virgins, whom his mild eyes rape.

So many dear distractions bother him,
Whose dreary inner eye must always be
Searching that fathomless and empty sea
Where music and sweet poetry agree
And innocent glad dolphins sometimes swim.

Poem For Oscar Wilde

Lane is cutting cucumber
Sandwiches, and the dogcart
Is coming round at the same
Time next week. The weather
Continues charming.

Reading Gaol and seedy France
Lurk in Cecily's garden
Under the pink roses. As
A man sows, so let him reap.
This truth is rarely pure,
And never simple.

Babies, handbags and lives are
Abandoned (I use the word
In the sense of *lost* or *mislaid*).
Sin, a temperance beverage,
Has stained somebody's lining.

This exquisite egg, which hatched
Ruin for you, who made it,
Retains its delicate poise.
Grief turns hair gold, and teacake
Can be tragic. The weather
Continues charming.

Only A Small Death

Only a small death, of course,
Not the full ceremony with mourners, a hearse,
Residuary legatees and a beanfeast
After the crematorium. Just a small, fully-
Conscious end.

Never again will you sleep in
This room, see sun rise through glass at this
Familiar angle, never again
Adjust to the shape of this bath, the smell
Of this cupboard.

You have died suddenly. The arrival
Of undertakers informs you of your
Decease. Their muscular detachment dissolves
Bonds between chairs and rooms, shelves
And their books.

The house offers its own valuation
Of the late owner. Dirt appears
In embarassing contexts. If you were still
Alive, you would feel the need
To apologise.

Casual adjuncts of ordinary
Living, dustbins and drains, the
Unremarkable milkman, haloed in
The otherworldly glare of the last rites,
Achieve reality

Just as you end with them for ever.
Neighbours, paying a deathbed visit,
Acquire the tender resonance of friends,
But die as you go, birth exists on the edge
Of extinction.

The heir, arriving tactlessly early,
Retires till you finish dying. With you go
Archaic patterns of a home you will never
Come home to. Like an amputation, it will
Haunt you in the grave.

Family Entertainment

A nice evening for it. The firemen
Look in their yellow helmets
Just like the seven dwarfs.

Blue sky, green trees, red fire.
The ladies in the crowd wear floral
Dresses and sandals, the children less.

The dogs are well-behaved, lying
On the grass and panting politely. We
Behave well, too, taking care

Not to block anyone's view. We don't
Intrude on the group by the ambulance,
We preserve a proper distance

From the hosepipes and sirens. Fresh
From kite-watching and ball-games,
With the same detached attention,

We eye ruin. The dwarfs with their axes
Hack at the stockbroker's gothic, hand
Smoking armchairs through crazed windows.

Ashy carpet flakes over sills,
Torches wink in bedrooms, the intercom
Mutters away to itself. A hose leaks.

A neighbour runs past with a basin
And towels. Some of us imagine
The losses and injuries, but no one

Cares to find out. We are simply
A crowd, whose part is to watch.
The house will be ready again

For tomorrow's performance, the wounds
Washed off. Only, as we wander away,
We sniff the scorching in our own kitchens.

Ridge House (Old People's Home)

Something dramatic ought to happen here.
These pools and pergolas, these long dim fish
Anticipate an entrance, and offstage
Butler and parlourmaid are polishing
Silver and dialogue impartially.
Edwardian high comedy, of course.
Epigrams fidget in the atmosphere.

The trees are close, too. Something might draw near
Under the dead beech leaves. A cloven foot
Moves otherwise than ours, and makes less noise.
The shadowed lawn looks knowing. Grass, of course,
Has contacts with the supernatural.
At night, perhaps, when no one is about,
Oberon's cavalry manoeuvre here.

But all's quiet now. The August sky is clear,
Wisteria hangs its leaflets undisturbed.
The weather and the garden both deserve
A compliment, but no one's here of course,
Except a sexless, ageless, shapeless shape,
Hunched underneath the cedar, muffled, rugged,
Which cannot see or smell, touch, taste or hear.

Dramatist to this house is Death. Austere,
Withdrawn, the scripts he writes. A single bed
Is his theatre. There the actor lies
Alone, and in the long dim hours explores
Dissolving senses. No one cares, of course.
The garden and the weather stay remote;
No god leaps from the clouds to interfere.

Men On Allotments

As mute as monks, tidy as bachelors,
They manicure their little plots of earth.
Pop music from the council house estate
Counterpoints with the Sunday-morning bells,
But neither siren voice has power for these
Drab solitary men who spend their time
Kneeling, or fetching water, soberly,
Or walking softly down a row of beans.

Like drill-sergeants, they measure their recruits.
The infant sprig receives the proper space
The manly fullgrown cauliflower will need.
And all must toe the line here; stem and leaf,
As well as root, obey the rule of string.
Domesticated tilth aligns itself
In sweet conformity; but head in air
Soars the unruly loveliness of beans.

They visit hidden places of the earth
When tenderly with fork and hand they grope
To lift potatoes, and the round, flushed globes
Tumble like pearls out of the moving soil.
They share strange intuitions, know how much
Patience and energy and sense of poise
It takes to be an onion; and they share
The subtle benediction of the beans.

They see the casual holiness that spreads
Along obedient furrows. Cabbages
Unfurl their veined and rounded fans in joy,
And buds of sprouts rejoice along their stalks.
The ferny tops of carrots, stout red stems
Of beetroot, zany sunflowers with blond hair
And bloodshot faces, shine like seraphim
Under the long flat fingers of the beans.

Pat At Milking Time

This enterprise is sick. The placid rats
Know it, roundhaunched and glossy, taking
Turns in the straw, like country dancers.

The dairy smells of defeat and sour milk.
Bank manager on Wednesday. Herb cheese
Drains peacefully through muslin into the churn.

The kids don't understand, knowing
Nothing but now, and the imperatives
Of suck, sleep, wriggle. In their world

It's normal to be fed at three o'clock
In the morning. What a field contains—
Sun, daisies, wind— is not to be imagined.

Growing up keeps them busy. But the milkers
Know, and are sad. They come to her pail
One by one, independently, as she calls them,

Christabel, Infanta, Treasure and *Nickel,*
Mosquito and *Gnat,* stepping thoughtfully,
Nibbling her straggly hair, weaving

Their sympathetic magic behind her back,
Watching through square-lensed eyes. Every day
There is less milk in their taut pronged teats.

Love is no help. Like cats they rub against her.
The church clock echoes oddly. The strident
Mew of a peacock slices the neutral air.

Canal: 1977

I remember this place: the conspiratorial
Presence of trees, the leaves' design
On uncommitted water, the pocky stonework
Ruining mildly in mottled silence,
The gutted pub, the dropping sounds
Inside the tunnel, I remember this place.

And before. I remember the sly lurchers,
The rose-and-castled barges, serious horses,
Coal smell, the leggers' hollow whoops
Down water, the bankrupt contractors
Grizzling into their beer, the trees and grass
Waiting to take over. I remember before.

And I remember the not-yet after,
When the money's raised and the sparetime Sunday
Navvying's over, the last intrusive sapling
Is ashes, when the bunting has bobbed, the first
Distinguished head ducked under the keystone,
There will be an after to be remembered

As the pleasurecraft purr their idle way
Into sunshine, and the smooth pink families
With their superior dogs enjoy the water,
The weather, the picturesque antiquity
That savaged so many who made it.
I remember after. And after

And before, the mute persistence of water
And grass and trees. Humanity goes out
Like a light, like the Roman-candle miners,
Shafting their pits on a donkey-winch, astraddle
A powderkeg, light in their teeth, a fuse in each pocket,
Lying foreign and broken in Gloucestershire churchyards now.

Horticultural Show

These are Persephone's fruits
Of the underyear. These will guide us
Through the slow dream of winter.

Onions her paleskinned lamps.
Rub them for strange knowledge. They shine
With the light of the tomb.

Drawn in fine runes along
Hard green rinds, the incomprehensible
Initiation of the marrow.

All orange energy driven
Down to a final hair, these carrots
Have been at the heart of darkness.

And parti-coloured leeks,
Their green hair plaited, like Iroquois braves,
Leaning exhausted in corners.

Holystoned the presence
Of potatoes, pure white and stained pink.
Persephone's bread.

Sacrificed beetroots
Display their bleeding hearts. We read
The future in these entrails.

Out in the world excitable
Ponies caper, Punch batters Judy, a man
Creates a drystone wall in thirty minutes,

Arrows fly, coconuts fall, crocodiles
And Jubilee mugs, disguised as children,
Cope with candyfloss, the band
Adds its slow waltz heart beat.

Here in the tent, in the sepia hush,
Persephone's fruits utter where they have been,
Where we are going.

Staff Party

Silky and bland, like Roman emperors,
With kiss-curls trained across their noble brows,
They sit, my colleagues, laughing in the right
Self-conscious way at all the proper points.

I've known them for so long, and yet I don't
Know them at all. I know their parlour tricks,
Their favourite cardigans and recipes,
Their hairdressers, their views about the split
Infinitive, the Principal and What
Is Wrong with Modern Parents, know the names
Of children, husbands, cats. I know that when
Some local battle clouds relationships
(Shoplifting, drugs, the press or pregnancy—
So many trivial things can go astray
Besides the bigger, permanent mishaps:
The timetable, or the supply of ink),
Some will orate, some help, and some betray.

We know what each will do. But some cold hand
Stops us from knowing more. That's dangerous,
Even disloyal. For already we
Know more than's proper about all of us.

We know our reputations and nicknames,
Enthusiast, digressor, confidante,
The one who just can't concentrate on girls
Because she's getting married, and the one
Who never does her washing. Emperors
Preserved their Roman calm in public life,
Unless they liked it otherwise, but these
Statuesque Romans have Suetonius
Around them all the time, scribbling on desks,
Asking discursive questions, argus-eyed,
Flypaper-memoried historians,
Publishing every moment of the day
Sober surmises and fantastic truth.

Knowing all this, and knowing we are known,
We must respect the anonymity
We decent ladies all pretend to have,
Letting the Whore, the Genius, the Witch,
The Slut, the Miser and the Psychopath
Go down to history, if they really must,
While Caesar keeps his bright precarious gloss.

Woman's World

They inhabit other
Worlds, these browsers
At the rack of magazines.

The gardener, the yachtsman,
Adrift in a world of tackle
And climbing begonias.

Their fingers move on the thick paper,
They are already there, in
The Channel, the bastard trench.

The cavey-breeder
Sees it all before him,
The impossible triumphs calmly achieved at shows,
Before he has even bought his magazine,
Let alone a guinea-pig.

Only the women fail
To enter this golden arena
Of dedicated action.

Their magazines offer
Not the single track of Amateur
Gardening, Motorboat
And Yachting, Cat-Fancier's Gazette,

Only the impossible junctions
Of being a woman.

Song

Don't eavesdrop on my heart,
    It's a sneak.
It will chat with any stranger,
Lifeguard, lover, doctor, tailor;
It just needs to feel an ear
    And it will speak.

Don't eavesdrop on my heart,
    It's illiterate.
The educated hand, eye, brain,
Turn words to shapes and back again;
My stupid heart could never learn
    The alphabet.

Don't eavesdrop on my heart,
    It's dumb.
In rainforests of tubes and pumps
It hangs, my heart, a third-world dunce;
Parrots can speak, but my heart just
    Communicates by drum.

Don't eavesdrop on my heart,
    It's clever.
And if your head should touch my breast
My heart would make its own arrest,
Develop hands, as trees grow leaves,
    And hold you there forever.

U.A. Fanthorpe writes: "I was born in Kent in 1929 of middle-class but honest parents and correctly educated at Oxford. After that I taught at Cheltenham, where diffidence and the need to turn an honest penny made it easy to forget such literary ambitions as I had had. Sixteen years later I decided that the day of dedication to the honest penny was over and I became a middle-aged drop-out in order to write. Since then I have been on the dole, worked as a temp., and lived in Merthyr Tydfil. Now I work fulltime as a clerk in a Bristol hospital, and live in Gloucestershire. Abandoning responsibility and Burnham scale in favour of a 9–5 job has somehow made it possible for me to write. My friends have been very nice about it.

Many of the poems in *Side Effects* were written during the lunch hour of my working day in a hospital, and inevitably many therefore spring from the experiences of work. But others owe their origin to the most ordinary experiences of everyday life. Some forced themselves upon me when I least expected them (often when it was inconvenient, too); others had to be stalked as gently and perseveringly as a rare bird."

Side Effects is U.A. Fanthorpe's first collection of poems. Poems within this collection have appeared in the following magazines and anthologies: *Encounter, Poetry Review, Use Of English, New Poetry 2* (Arts Council), *P.E.N. New Poems, 1977-78, Poetry Dimension Annual 5.* 'Men On Allotments' won first prize in the *Michael Johnson Memorial Competition* (1976); 'My Brother's House' was joint second in the *Stroud International Poetry Competition* (1976); 'Not My Best Side' won second prize in the *Poem About A Painting* competition organized by *Phoenix* magazine in 1975.